In the Year 1983

by

Kerry Butters

In the Year 1983

Millennium: 2nd millennium

Centuries: 19th century – **20th century** – 21st century

Decades: 1950s 1960s 1970s – **1980s** – 1990s 2000s 2010s

Years: 1980 1981 1982 – **1983** – 1984 1985 1986

1983 (MCMLXXXIII)was a common year starting on Saturday (dominical letter B) of the Gregoriancalendar, the 1983rd year of the Common Era (CE) and*Anno Domini* (AD) designations, the 983rd year of the 2nd millennium, the 83rd year of the 20th century, and the 4th year of the 1980s decade.

The year **1983** saw both the official beginning of the Internet and the first mobile cellular telephone call.

Contents

Events

January

- January 1 – The migration of the ARPANET to TCP/IP is officially completed (this is considered to be the beginning of the true Internet).
- January 3 – Kīlauea begins slowly erupting on the Big Island of Hawaii and is still flowing as of 2016.
- January 10 – Canada, the United Kingdom and the United States launch *Fraggle Rock*, a worldwide program advocating peace.
- January 19 – High-ranking Nazi war criminal Klaus Barbie is arrested in Bolivia.
- January 24 – Twenty-five members of the Red Brigades are sentenced to life imprisonment for the 1978 murder of Aldo Moro.
- January 25 – IRAS is launched from Vandenberg AFB, to conduct the world's first all-sky infrared survey from space.
- January 26 – Lotus 1-2-3 is released for IBM PC compatible computers.
- January 31 – Seatbelt use for drivers and front seat passengers becomes mandatory in the United Kingdom.

February

- February 2 – Giovanni Vigliotto goes on trial for multiple counts of bigamy involving 105 women.
- February 3 – Australian Prime Minister Malcolm Fraser is granted a double dissolution of both houses of parliament, for elections the next day.

- February 3 – Bob Hawke replaces Bill Hayden as leader of the Australian Labor Party.
- February 6 – Klaus Barbie is officially charged with war crimes.
- February 12 – 100 women protest in Lahore, Pakistan, against military dictator Zia-ul-Haq's proposed Law of Evidence. The women were tear-gassed, baton-charged and thrown into lock-up. The women were successful in repealing the law.
- February 13 – A cinema fire in Turin, Italy, kills 64 people.
- February 16 – The Ash Wednesday bushfires in Victoria and South Australia claim the lives of 75 people, in one of Australia's worst bushfire disasters.
- February 18
  - The Venezuelan bolívar is devaluated and exchange controls are established in an event now referred to as *Black Friday* by many Venezuelans (the Bolívar had been the most stable and internationally accepted currency).
  - Nellie massacre: Over 2,000 people, mostly Bangladeshi Muslims, are massacred in Assam, India, during the Assam agitation.
  - Wah Mee massacre: 13 people are killed in an attempted robbery in Seattle, Washington.
- February 23
  - The United States Environmental Protection Agency announces its intention to buy out and evacuate the dioxin-contaminated community of Times Beach, Missouri.
  - The automatic shut-down fails at Salem Nuclear Power Plant, New Jersey, USA.
- February 24
  - A special commission of the Congress of the United States releases a report critical of the practice of Japanese internment during World War II.
  - Bermondsey by-election, 1983 (U.K.): Simon Hughes's defeat of Peter Tatchell is criticised for alleged homophobia.
- February 28 – The final episode of *M*A*S*H* airs, setting a record for most watched television episode and reaching a total audience estimated at 125 million.

March

- March 1 – The Balearic Islands and Madrid become Autonomous communities of Spain.
- March 5 – Bob Hawke is elected Prime Minister of Australia, ending over 7 years of Conservative rule under Malcolm Fraser.
- March 8 – IBM releases the IBM PC XT.
- March 9
  - Anne Burford resigns as head of the United States Environmental Protection Agency amid scandal.
  - The 3D printer is invented by Chuck Hull.
- March 11 – Australia's First Hawke Ministry is sworn in; Andrew Peacock becomes Federal Opposition leader.
- March 16 – The Ismaning radio transmitter (last wooden radio tower in Germany) is demolished.
- March 23 – Strategic Defense Initiative: U.S. President Ronald Reagan makes his initial proposal to develop technology to intercept enemy missiles. The media dub this plan "Star Wars".
- March 25 – Motown celebrates its 25th anniversary with the television special *Motown 25: Yesterday, Today, Forever*, during which Michael Jackson performs "Billie Jean" and introduces the moonwalk.

April

- April 4 – First flight of the Space Shuttle Challenger.
- April 13 – California's largest retailer Target Corporation expands into California, opening 11 stores.
- April 15 – Tokyo Disneyland opens.
- April 18
  - The 1983 United States embassy bombing in Beirut kills 63 people.
  - Channel broadcasting is founded by Disney (the Disney Channel).
- April 22 – A reactor shut-down due to failure of fuel rods occurs at Kursk Nuclear Power Plant, Russia.

- April 25 – Manchester, Maine, US, schoolgirl Samantha Smith is invited to visit the Soviet Union by its leader Yuri Andropov, after he read her letter in which she expressed fears about nuclear war.

May

- May 6 – *Stern* magazine publishes the "Hitler Diaries" (which are later found to be forgeries).
- May 11 – Aberdeen F.C. beat Real Madrid 2–1 (after extra time) to win the European Cup Winners' Cup in 1983 and become only the third Scottish side to win a European trophy.
- May 14 – Dundee United F.C. are crowned Champions of Scotland for the first time in their history by winning the Scottish Premier League, on the final day of the league season at the home of their city rivals Dundee F.C. at Dens Park.
- May 16 – NSW Premier Neville Wran steps down, in response to allegations raised by the ABC program *Four Corners*, that he attempted to influence the NSW Magistracy.
- May 17 – Lebanon, Israel, and the United States sign an agreement on Israeli withdrawal from Lebanon.
- May 20
  - Two separate research groups led by Robert Gallo and Luc Montagnier independently declared that a novel retrovirus may have been infecting people with HIV/AIDS, and published their findings in the same issue of the journal *Science*.
  - Church Street bombing, a car bombing in Pretoria South Africa kills 19 people. It had been planted by members of Umkhonto we Sizwe, a military wing of the African National Congress.
- May 25 – *Return of the Jedi* opens in theatres.
- May 26 – The 7.8 Mw Sea of Japan earthquake shakes northern Honshu with a maximum Mercalli intensity of VIII (*Severe*). A destructive tsunami is generated that leaves about 100 people dead.

- May 27 – Benton fireworks disaster, an explosion at an unlicensed fireworks operation near Benton, Tennessee kills eleven, injures one, and causes damage within a radius of five miles.
- May 28 – The 9th G7 summit begins at Williamsburg, Virginia.
- May 29 – Tom Sneva wins the Indianapolis 500
- May 31 – The Philadelphia 76ers defeat the LA Lakers to sweep the NBA championship in four games.

June

- June – Throughout the local summer – Many Midwestern American states are affected by a severe drought that causes water shortages.
- June 9 – Britain's Conservative government, led by Margaret Thatcher, is re-elected by a landslide majority.
- June 13 – *Pioneer 10* passes the orbit of Neptune, becoming the first man-made object to leave the vicinity of the major planets of the Solar System.
- June 16 – Cork Graham is caught off the Vietnamese island of Phú Quốc looking for treasure buried by Captain Kidd. He is convicted and imprisoned until 1984 for illegal entry.
- June 18
  - Sally Ride becomes the first American woman in space aboard Space Shuttle *Challenger* on the STS-7 mission.
  - Iranian teenager Mona Mahmudnizhad and nine other women are hanged because of their membership of the Bahá'í Faith.
- June 19 – Dragon's Lair is released in arcades.
- June 25 – India wins the Cricket World Cup by defeating the West Indies by 43 runs.
- June 30 – A total loss of coolant occurs at the Embalse Nuclear Power Station, Argentina. It is classified as an "Accident With Local Consequences" – level 4 on the International Nuclear Event Scale.

July

- July 1
  - A North Korean Ilyushin Il-62M jet, en route to Conakry Airport in Guinea, crashes into the Fouta Djall Mountains in Guinea-Bissau, killing all 23 people on board.
  - The High Court of Australia blocks construction of the Franklin Dam in Tasmania.
  - A technical failure causes the release of iodine-131 from the Philippsburg Nuclear Power Plant, Germany.
- July 15
  - Nintendo's Family Computer, also known as the Famicom, goes on sale in Japan.
  - The Orly Airport attack in Paris leaves 8 dead and 55 injured.
- July 16 – Sikorsky S-61 disaster: A helicopter crashes off the Isles of Scilly, causing 20 fatalities.
- July 20 – The government of Poland announces the end of martial law and amnesty for political prisoners.
- July 21 – The lowest temperature on Earth is recorded in Vostok Station, Antarctica with −89.2 °C (−128.6 °F).
- July 22 – Australian Dick Smith completes his solo circumnavigation in a helicopter.
- July 23
  - Gimli Glider: Out of fuel, Air Canada Flight 143 glides in to land in Gimli, Manitoba.
  - 13 Sri Lanka Army soldiers are killed after a deadly ambush by the militant Liberation Tigers of Tamil Eelam, starting the Sri Lankan Civil War which continued until 2009.
  - Heavy massive rain and mudslides at western Shimane Prefecture, Japan, kill 117.
- July 24 – The Black July anti-Tamil riots begin in Sri Lanka, killing between 400 and 3,000. Black July is generally regarded as the beginning of the Sri Lankan Civil War.
- July 28 – New South Wales premier Neville Wran is exonerated by the Street Royal Commission, over claims raised by the ABC

(Australian Broadcasting Corporation) programme *Four Corners*, that he attempted to influence the NSW magistracy.

August

- August 1 – America West Airlines begins operations out of Phoenix, Arizona and Las Vegas, Nevada.
- August 4 – Thomas Sankara becomes President of Upper Volta.
- August 16 – *The Bill* first airs as *Woodentop*.
- August 18
  - Hurricane Alicia hits the Texas coast, killing 22 and causing over US$3.8 billion (2005 dollars) in damage.
  - Five people are killed and 18 others injured when a road train is deliberately driven into a motel at Ayers Rock, NT (the driver, Douglas Edward Crabbe, is convicted in March 1984).
- August 21 – Benigno Aquino, Jr., Philippines opposition leader, is assassinated in Manila just as he returns from exile.

August 21: Philippines opposition leader Benigno Aquino, Jr. is assassinated at Manila International Airport.

- August 24 – The Old Philadelphia Arena is destroyed by arson.
- August 26 – Heavy rain triggers flooding at Bilbao, Spain, and surrounding areas, killing 45 people and causing millions in damages.

- August 30 – Guion Bluford becomes the first African-American in space aboard Space Shuttle *Challenger* on the STS-8 mission.

September

- September 1 – Cold War: Korean Air Lines Flight 007 is shot down by Soviet Union Air Force Su-15 Flagon pilot Major Gennadi Osipovich near Moneron Island when the commercial aircraft enters Soviet airspace. All 269 on board are killed including U.S. Congressman Larry McDonald.
- September 4 – Six men walk underwater across Sydney Harbour – 82.9 km in 48 hours.
- September 6 – The Soviet Union admits to shooting down Korean Air Lines Flight 007, stating that the pilots did not know it was a civilian aircraft when it violated Soviet airspace.
- September 9 – Iraqi club Al-Shorta wins the 1983 President's Gold Cup by defeating Malaysia 2-0 in the final.
- September 16 – President Ronald Reagan announces that the Global Positioning System (GPS) will be made available for civilian use.
- September 17 – Vanessa L. Williams becomes the first African American to be crowned Miss America, in Atlantic City, New Jersey.
- September 18 – U.S. heavy metal band Kiss officially appears in public without makeup for the first time on MTV.
- September 19
  - Saint Kitts and Nevis becomes an independent state.
  - *Wheel of Fortune* begins its syndicated version, which still churns out new episodes to this very day.
- September 23
  - Gulf Air Flight 771 crashes in the United Arab Emirates after a bomb explodes in the baggage compartment, killing 117.
  - Violence erupts in New Caledonia between native Kanaks and French expatriates. The French government withdraws the promise of independence.

- September 24 – U.S. rock group the Red Hot Chili Peppers launch their first self-titled album.
- September 25 – Maze Prison escape: 38 Provisional Irish Republican Army prisoners, armed with 6 handguns, hijack a prison lorry and smash their way out of HM Prison Maze in Northern Ireland, in the largest prison escape since World War II and in British history.
- September 26
  - 1983 Soviet nuclear false alarm incident: Soviet military officer Stanislav Petrov averts a worldwide nuclear war by correctly identifying a warning of attack by U.S. missiles as a false alarm.
  - The *Soyuz T-10-1* mission ends in a pad abort at the Baikonur Cosmodrome, when a pad fire occurs at the base of the Soyuz U rocket during the launch countdown. The escape tower system, attached to the top of the capsule containing the crew and Soyuz spacecraft, fires immediately, pulling the crew safe from the vehicle a few seconds before the rocket explodes, destroying the launch complex.
  - The Australian yacht *Australia II* wins the America's Cup, the first successful challenge to the New York Yacht Club's 132-year defence of the sailing trophy.
- September 27 – The GNU Project is announced publicly on the net.unix-wizards and net.usoft newsgroups.

October

- October 2 – Neil Kinnock is elected leader of the British Labour Party.
- October 4 – British entrepreneur Richard Noble sets a new land speed record of 633.468 mph (1,019.468 km/h), driving Thrust2 at the Black Rock Desert, Nevada.
- October 4 – The first Hooters opened in Clearwater, Florida.
- October 7 – A plan to abolish the Greater London Council is announced.

- October 9 – The Rangoon bombing kills South Korea's Foreign Minister, Lee Bum Suk, and 21 others. The perpetrators are believed to be North Koreans.
- October 12 – Japan's former Prime Minister Kakuei Tanaka is found guilty of taking a $2 million bribe from Lockheed, and sentenced to 4 years in jail.
- October 19 – Maurice Bishop, Prime Minister of Grenada, and 40 others are assassinated in a military coup.
- October 21 – At the 17th General Conference on Weights and Measures, the metre is defined in terms of the speed of light as the distance light travels in a vacuum in 1/299,792,458 of a second.
- October 22 – In Bonn, West Germany, people demonstrate for nuclear disarmament.
- October 23 – Beirut barracks bombing: Simultaneous suicide truck-bombings destroy both the French Army and United States Marine Corps barracks in Beirut, killing 241 U.S. servicemen, 58 French paratroopers and 6 Lebanese civilians.
- October 25 – Invasion of Grenada by United States troops at the behest of Eugenia Charles of Dominica, a member of the Organization of American States.
- October 30 – Argentine general election: The first democratic elections in Argentina after 7 years of military rule are held.

November

- November 2
  - Martin Luther King, Jr. Day: At the White House Rose Garden, U.S. President Ronald Reagan signs a bill creating a federal holiday on the third Monday of every January to honor American civil rights leader Martin Luther King Jr. It is first observed in 1986.
  - Able Archer 83: Many Soviet officials misinterpret this NATO exercise as a nuclear first strike, causing the last nuclear scare of the Cold War.

- South Africa approves a new constitution granting limited political rights to Coloureds and Asians as part of a series of reforms to apartheid.
- Chrysler introduces the Dodge Caravan, the first "minivan".
- November 3 – The Reverend Jesse Jackson announces his candidacy for the 1984 United States' Democratic Party presidential nomination.
- November 5 – Byford Dolphin rig diving bell accident: Off the coast of Norway, 5 divers are killed and one severely wounded in an explosive decompression accident.
- November 10 – The anticancer drug etoposide is approved by the FDA, leading to a curative treatment regime in the field of combination chemotherapy of testicular carcinoma.
- November 11 – Ronald Reagan becomes the first U.S. President to address the National Diet, Japan's national legislature.
- November 13 – The first United States cruise missiles arrive at RAF Greenham Common in England amid protests from peace campaigners.
- November 14
  - The immunosuppressant cyclosporine is approved by the FDA, leading to a revolution in the field of transplantation.
  - Ecuador recognizes the Sahrawi Arab Democratic Republic (SADR).
- November 15 – The Turkish part of Cyprus declares independence.
- November 16 – A jury in Gretna, Louisiana, US acquits Ginny Foat of the murder of Argentine businessman Moses Chaiyo.
- November 17 – The Zapatista Army of National Liberation is founded in Mexico.
- November 19 – An attempted hijacking of Aeroflot Flight 6833 in Soviet Georgia results in several dead and wounded.
- November 20 – *The Day After* airs on ABC.
- November 24 – Lynda Mann, 15, is found raped and strangled in the village of Narborough, England (Colin Pitchfork is sentenced to life imprisonment in 1988).
- November 26 – Brink's-Mat robbery: In London, 6,800 gold bars worth nearly UK£26 million are taken from the Brink's-Mat vault

at Heathrow Airport. Only a fraction of the gold is ever recovered, and only 2 men are convicted of the crime.
- November 27 – Colombian Avianca Flight 11 crashes near Barajas Airport in Madrid, Spain, killing 181 of the 192 on board.

December

- December 2
  - Michael Jackson's Thriller video is aired on MTV for the first time.
- December 4
  - United States Navy aviator Lt's. Mark Lange and Bobby Goodman are shot down in an A-6 Intruder over Lebanon and captured by Syrians; Lt. Lange dies of his injuries; Lt. Goodman is released 30 days later after the intervention of the Reverend Jesse Jackson.
  - General elections are celebrated in Venezuela in which the opposition party, Democratic Action, wins a majority in both chambers of the Venezuelan Congress and the presidency for the 1984-1989 period under Jaime Lusinchi. Voter turn out is 87.3% and Lusinchi obtains 58.4% of the votes.
  - Solar eclipse of December 4, 1983.
- December 5 – ICIMOD is established and inaugurated with its headquarters in Kathmandu, Nepal, and legitimised through an Act of Parliament in Nepal this same year.
- December 7 – Two Spanish passenger planes collide on the foggy runway at a Madrid airport, killing 90.
- December 9 – The Australian dollar is floated, by Federal treasurer Paul Keating. Under the old flexible peg system, the Reserve Bank bought and sold all Australian dollars and cleared the market at the end of the day. This initiative is taken by the government of Bob Hawke.
- December 10 – Military rule ends and democracy is restored in Argentina, with the beginning of Raúl Alfonsín's first term as President of Argentina

- December 13 – Turgut Özal, of ANAP forms the new government of Turkey (45th government); beginning of a new civilian regime
- December 17
  - A discotheque fire in Madrid, Spain, kills 83 people.
  - A Provisional IRA car bomb kills 6 Christmas shoppers and injures 90 outside Harrods in London.
- December 19 – The Jules Rimet Trophy is stolen from the Brazilian Soccer Confederation building in Rio de Janeiro. As of 2016, the trophy has not been recovered.
- December 27
  - A propane explosion in Buffalo, New York, US kills 5 firefighters and 2 civilians.
  - Pope John Paul II visits Rebibbia prison to forgive his would-be assassin Mehmet Ali Ağca.
- December 29 – The Reverend Jesse Jackson travels to Syria to secure the release of U.S. Navy Lieutenant Robert Goodman, who has been in Syrian captivity since being shot down over Lebanon during a bombing mission.
- December 31
  - Brunei gains independence from the United Kingdom.
  - Two bombs explode in France; one on the Paris train kills 3 and injures 19. The other at Marseille station kills 2 and injures 34.

Date unknown

- I. M. Pei wins the Pritzker Architecture Prize.
- Zlatko Ugljen receives the Aga Khan Award for Architecture for Šerefudin's White Mosque, built in Visoko.
- The Drug Abuse Resistance Education (DARE) program is launched in the U.S.
- *Flashdance* and *Return of the Jedi* are box-office hits.
- Gérard Debreu wins the Nobel Memorial Prize in Economic Sciences.
- Kellogg's introduces *Crispix* cereal.

- Leopold Kohr, the people of Belau, Amory and Hunter Lovins / Rocky Mountain Institute and Manfred Max Neef / CEPAUR win the Right Livelihood Award.
- McDonald's introduces the *McNugget*.
- Kary Mullis discovers polymerase chain reaction while working for Cetus.
- The DeLorean Motor Company ceases production.
- The meteorological El Niño phenomenon brings severe weather worldwide.
- Ronald Reagan declassifies GPS for public use; it will be shut down again in 1990 for the Gulf War and re-activated again in 1993.
- The capital of the Republic of Côte d'Ivoire is changed from Abidjan to Yamoussoukro.

Births

January

Kim Jong Un

Kate Bosworth

Chris Getzlaf

- January 1 – Calum Davenport, English footballer
- January 2 – Kate Bosworth, American actress
- January 3 – Precious Lara Quigaman, Filipina model, host and actress
- January 4 – Spencer Chamberlain, American musician
- January 6 – Cristina Rosato, Canadian actress
- January 7
  - Natalie Gulbis, American golfer
  - Robert Ri'chard, American actor
  - Tosin Abasi, Nigerian-American musician (Animals As Leaders)
- January 8
  - Chris Masters, American wrestler

- Chen Xiexia, Chinese weightlifter
  - Kim Jong-un, Supreme Leader of North Korea
- January 9
  - Gala Évora, Spanish actress
  - Kerry Condon, Irish television and film actress
  - Chris Getzlaf, American football player; brother of Anaheim Ducks captain Ryan Getzlaf
- January 10 – Li Nina, Chinese aerial free-style skier
- January 11 – Adrian Sutil, German Formula One driver
- January 12 – Shawn Desman, Canadian singer
- January 13
  - Brianne Moncrief, American soap opera actress
  - Ronny Turiaf, French basketball player
  - Imran Khan, Indian actor
  - Julian Morris, British actor
- January 14 – Takako Uehara, Japanese singer
- January 15 – Kaine Bennett Charleston, Australian film producer, film and stage actor
- January 16
  - Marwan Kenzari, Dutch actor
  - Emanuel Pogatetz, Austrian footballer
- January 17 – Johannes Herber, German basketball player
- January 18
  - Jelena Gavrilović, Serbian actress
  - Samantha Mumba, Irish singer and actress
- January 19 – Hikaru Utada, Japanese singer and songwriter
- January 20
  - Geovany Soto, Puerto Rican baseball player
  - Yasser Elshantaf, Palestinian entrepreneur
- January 21
  - Maryse, French-Canadian professional wrestler and glamour model
  - Svetlana Khodchenkova, Russian actress
  - Moritz Volz, German footballer
- January 22 – Shaun Cody, American football player
-

- January 23
  - David Firth, British animator
  - Justyna Kowalczyk, Polish cross-country skier
  - Sarah Tait, Australian rower (d. 2016)
- January 24
  - Scott Speed, American Formula One driver
  - Diane Birch, American singer-songwriter
  - Teo, Belarusian singer
- January 25 – Yasuyuki Konno, Japanese footballer
- January 27 – Rebecca Judd, Australian model and television presenter
- January 31
  - James Sutton, British actor
  - Belçim Bilgin, Turkish actress

February

Emily Blunt

Kate Mara

- February 1 – Andrew VanWyngarden, American singer
- February 2
  - Carolina Klüft, Swedish athlete
  - David Call, American film and television actor
- February 3
  - Hillary Scott, American pornographic actress
  - Damiel Dossévi, French pole vaulter
  - Gabriel Sargissian, Armenian chess Grandmaster
- February 5 – Vanessa Rousso, French-American professional poker player
- February 6
  - Michael Robinson, former American football player
  - Sreesanth, Indian cricketer
- February 7
  - Scott Feldman, American baseball player
  - Elin Grindemyr, Swedish model
- February 8
  - Atiba Hutchinson, Canadian footballer
  - Louise Glover, English model and photographer
  - Olga Syahputra, Indonesian actor, comedian, singer, and television presenter (d. 2015)
  - Ashley Mulheron, Scottish actress and television presenter
- February 11 – Rafael van der Vaart, Dutch footballer
- February 15
  - Alan Didak, Australian rules footballer
  - Philipp Degen and David Degen, Swiss footballers
  - Russell Martin, Canadian baseball player
  - Selita Ebanks, Caymanian model
- February 16
  - Agyness Deyn, English supermodel
  - John Magaro, American film, television and stage actor
- February 17
  - Kevin Rudolf, American singer-songwriter and record producer
  - Elin Kling, Swedish fashion journalist
- February 18 – Jason Maxiell, American basketball player

- February 19
  - Kotoōshū Katsunori (Kaloyan Mahlyanov), Bulgarian sumo wrestler
  - Ryan Whitney, American ice hockey player
  - Nozomi Sasaki, Japanese voice actress
  - Mika Nakashima, Japanese singer and actress
- February 20
  - Justin Verlander, American baseball player
  - Emad Moteab, Egyptian footballer
- February 21
  - Mélanie Laurent, French actress and director
  - Eoin Macken, Irish actor
- February 22
  - Penny Flame, born Jennifer Ketcham, American former pornographic actress/reality TV star
  - Iliza Shlesinger, American comedian
- February 23
  - Mirco Bergamasco, Italian rugby union player
  - Mido, Egyptian footballer
  - Emily Blunt, English actress
  - Aziz Ansari, American comedian and actor
- February 24 – Sophie Howard, English glamour model
- February 25 – Eduardo da Silva, Croatian soccer player
- February 26 – Andrew Baggaley, English table tennis player
- February 27
  - Devin Harris, American basketball player
  - Kate Mara, American television and film actress
  - Hayley Angel Holt, English actress
  - Vítězslav Veselý, Czech javelin thrower
- February 28 – Linda Király, American-Hungarian singer-songwriter

March

Lee Ha-nui

Carrie Underwood

Mo Farah

- March 2 – Lee Ha-nui, South Korean beauty pageant titleholder, classical musician, and actress
- March 3
  - Katie White, English singer (The Ting Tings)
  - Kim Smith, American fashion model and actress
- March 4
  - Samuel Contesti, Italian figure skater
  - Jessica Heap, American actress
  - Adam Deacon, British actor
- March 7 – Raquel Alessi, American actress
- March 9
  - Bryony Afferson, English actress and musician
  - Maite Perroni, Mexican singer and actress
  - Clint Dempsey, American footballer
  - Bobby Campo, American actor
- March 10
  - Janet Mock, American author and activist
  - Jonas Olsson, Swedish footballer
  - Aimee Walker Pond, American gymnast
  - Rafe Spall, English actor
  - Carrie Underwood, American singer
- March 11 – Melissa Rycroft, American television personality and reality television contestant
- March 14
  - Bakhtiyar Artayev, Kazakh boxer
  - Taylor Hanson, American musician (Hanson)
- March 15 – Florencia Bertotti, Argentine actress and singer
- March 16
  - Stephanie Gatschet, American actress
  - Katie Kim, Irish singer-songwriter
- March 17
  - Penny McNamee, Australian actress
  - Atit Shah, Indian American Hollywood film producer
- March 19 – Nicole Muirbrook, American actress and model
- March 20
  - Eiji Kawashima, Japanese footballer

- ○ Jenni Vartiainen, Finnish pop singer
- March 21 – Bruno Langley, British actor
- March 22
  - ○ Heather Lind, American actress
  - ○ Christina Bennett Lind, American actress
- March 23 – Mo Farah, British athlete
- March 27 – Shawntinice Polk, American basketball player (d. 2005)
- March 29 – Ezgi Mola, Turkish actress
- March 30
  - ○ Zach Gowen, American wrestler
  - ○ Hebe Tien, Taiwanese singer
- March 31
  - ○ Meinir Gwilym, Welsh folk singer
  - ○ Hashim Amla, South African cricketer
  - ○ Melissa Ordway, American actress and model

April

Sergey Lazarev

Jamie Chung

Francis Capra

- April 1
  - Ellen Hollman, American actress
  - Sean Taylor, American football player (d. 2007)
  - Matt Lanter, American actor and model
  - Sergey Lazarev, Russian pop-singer
- April 2 – Yung Joc, American rapper
- April 4
  - Doug Lynch, Canadian ice hockey player
  - Amanda Righetti, American actress and film producer
- April 6 – Diora Baird, American actress
- April 7 – Franck Ribéry, French footballer
- April 10
  - Jamie Chung, American actress
  - Ryan Merriman, American actor
- April 11 – Joanna Douglas, Canadian actress

- April 12
  - Jelena Dokić, Australian tennis player
  - Jonti Richter, Australian soccer player
  - Judy Marte, American actress and producer
- April 13 – Schalk Burger, South African rugby player
- April 15
  - Ilya Kovalchuk, Russian ice hockey player
  - Alice Braga, Brazilian actress
  - Matt Cardle, English singer-songwriter and guitarist
  - Siobhan Hewlett, Irish film, television and theatre actress
- April 16 – Alex Antônio de Melo Santos, Brazilian footballer
- April 18 – Miguel Cabrera, Venezuelan baseball player
- April 19
  - Joe Mauer, American baseball player
  - Curtis Thigpen, American baseball player
  - Alberto Callaspo, American baseball player
- April 20
  - Joanne King, Irish film and television actress
  - Miranda Kerr, Australian model
  - Sebastian Ingrosso, Swedish club DJ
- April 21
  - Tarvaris Jackson, American football player
  - Paweł Brożek, Polish footballer
- April 22
  - Matt Jones, American football player
  - Francis Capra, American actor
- April 23
  - Daniela Hantuchová, Slovakian tennis player
  - Aaron Hill, American actor
  - Hayley-Marie Coppin, English glamour model
- April 24 – Will Champlin, American singer, contestant from The Voice season 5
- April 29
  - Jay Cutler, American football player
  - Megan Boone, American actress
  - David Lee, American basketball player

- ○ Yuriko Shiratori, Japanese actress and gravure idol
- April 30 – Yelena Leuchanka, Belarusian professional women's basketball player

May

Henry Cavill

Adrianne Palicki

Amber Tamblyn

Nancy Ajram

- May 1 – Alain Bernard, French swimmer
- May 2
  - Dani Sordo, Spanish rally driver
  - Tina Maze, Slovenian alpine ski racer
- May 4 – Jesse Moss, Canadian actor
- May 5 – Henry Cavill, British actor
- May 6
  - Raquel Zimmermann, Brazilian model
  - Gabourey Sidibe, American actress
  - Adrianne Palicki, American actress
- May 9 – Ryuhei Matsuda, Japanese actor
- May 11
  - Matt Leinart, American football player
  - Holly Valance, Australian actress and singer
  - Daizee Haze, American professional wrestler
- May 12
  - Alicja Bachleda-Curuś, Polish actress and singer
  - Charilaos Pappas, Greek footballer
- May 13
  - Yaya Touré, Ivorian footballer
  - Natalie Cassidy, British actress
  - Anita Görbicz, Hungarian handball player
  - Grégory Lemarchal, French singer (d. 2007)
  -

- May 14
  - Amber Tamblyn, American actress
  - Anahí, Mexican singer and actress
  - Sarbel, Greek Cypriot pop singer
- May 16
  - Daniel Kerr, Australian rules footballer
  - Nancy Ajram, Lebanese singer
- May 17 – Channing Frye, American basketball player
- May 18 – Vince Young, American football player
- May 19
  - Eve Angel, Hungarian model
  - Jessica Fox, British actress
- May 20
  - Michaela McManus, American actress
  - Emma Williams, English stage and television actress
  - N. T. Rama Rao Jr., Indian actor and singer
- May 21 – Leva Bates, American professional wrestler
- May 22
  - John Hopkins, American MotoGP racer
  - Connie and Cassie Powney, English twin actresses
- May 23 – Heidi Range, British singer (Sugababes)
- May 24 – Woo Seung-yeon, South Korean actress and model
- May 27 – Bobby Convey, American soccer player
- May 28 – Toby Hemingway, British/American actor
- May 30 – Jennifer Ellison, British actress
- May 31
  - David Hernandez, American singer
  - Zana Marjanović, Bosnian actress

June

Alsou

Brooke White

Marina Lizorkina

Julia Fischer

Macklemore

- June 1 – Sylvia Hoeks, Dutch actress
- June 2 – Brooke White, American singer
- June 3 – Janine Carmen Habeck, German model
- June 6
  - Joe Rokocoko, New Zealand rugby union player
  - Gemma Bissix, British actress
  - Adam Hendershott, American actor
  - Gianna Michaels, porn actress
- June 7 – Indiggo, Romanian-born American twin sisters, singer-songwriters, and reality TV personalities
- June 8
  - Kim Clijsters, Belgian tennis player
  - Mamoru Miyano, Japanese voice actor
- June 9 – Marina Lizorkina, Russian singer (Serebro)
- June 10
  - Marina Abrosimova, Russian pop singer
  - Shanna Collins, American actress
  - Leelee Sobieski, American film and television actress
- June 11 – José Reyes, Dominican baseball player
- June 12
  - Andy Ologun, Nigerian mixed martial artist
  - Anja Rubik, Polish model
  - Bryan Habana, South African rugby union player
- June 13 – Jason Spezza, Canadian hockey player
- June 14
  - Torrance Coombs, Canadian film, theatre and television actor

- o Sean Klitzner, American internet personality and comedian
- June 15
  - o Julia Fischer, German violinist and pianist
  - o Derek Anderson, American football player
- June 16
  - o Verónica Echegui, Spanish actress
  - o Lisa Yamanaka, Canadian voice actress
- June 17
  - o Connie Fisher, British actress and singer
  - o Kazunari Ninomiya, Japanese actor, idol, and singer
  - o Lee Ryan, English singer (Blue)
- June 19
  - o Tanja Mihhailova, Russian-Estonian pop singer and actress
  - o Laura Norton, English actress
  - o Aidan Turner, Irish actor
  - o Mark Selby, British snooker player
  - o Macklemore, American rapper
- June 20 – Cherrie Ying, Hong Kong actress
- June 21
  - o Edward Snowden, American computer professional
  - o Jussie Smollett, American actor and singer
- June 22 – Sally Nicholls, English children's book author of *Ways to Live Forever*
- June 23 – Miles Fisher, American film and television actor and musician
- June 24
  - o John Lloyd Cruz, Filipino actor
  - o Shermain Jeremy, Antiguan singer and beauty pageant contestant
- June 25 – Cleo, Polish singer
- June 27 – Alsou, Russian singer, Eurovision Song Contest 2000 runner-up
- June 30
  - o Cheryl, British singer (Girls Aloud) and TV personality
  - o Katherine Ryan, Canadian comedian and actress

July

Michelle Branch

Katrina Kaif

- July 1
  - Park Jeong-su, Korean singer (Super Junior)
  - Marit Larsen, Norwegian singer and songwriter
  - Tanya Chisholm, American actress and dancer
- July 2
  - Michelle Branch, American singer (The Wreckers)
  - Alicia Menendez, American television commentator
- July 3 – Edinson Volquez, Dominican baseball player
- July 4 – Isabeli Fontana, Brazilian fashion model
-

- July 5
  - Zheng Jie, Chinese tennis player
  - Kumiko Ogura, Japanese badminton player
  - Edwina Bartholomew, Australian journalist and television presenter
- July 6 – Gregory Smith, Canadian actor
- July 10 – Kim Heechul, Korean actor and singer (Super Junior)
- July 11 – Marie Eleonor Serneholt, Swedish singer (A*Teens)
- July 12
  - Megumi Kawamura, Japanese model
  - Krystin Pellerin, Canadian actress of theatre, television and film
- July 13 – Liu Xiang, Chinese athlete
- July 15 – Maxim Dondyuk, Ukrainian documentary photographer
- July 16
  - Katrina Kaif, Bollywood actress and model
  - Zhang Xiangxiang, Chinese weightlifter
- July 17 – Flávia de Oliveira, Brazilian model
- July 19 – Helen Skelton, British television presenter
- July 21
  - Vinessa Antoine, Canadian actress
  - Eivør Pálsdóttir, Faroese singer and composer
  - Kellen Winslow II, American football player
- July 22
  - Juliana Felisberta, Brazilian beach volleyball player
  - Jodi Albert, English actress and singer
  - Sharni Vinson, Australian model, actress and dancer
  - Ifan Evans, Welsh rugby union player
- July 23
  - Aaron Peirsol, American swimmer
  - Bec Hewitt, Australian actress
- July 24
  - Daniele De Rossi, Italian footballer
  - Asami Mizukawa, Japanese actress
- July 26 – Elettra Weidemann, American fashion model and sociallite

- July 29
  - Kaitlyn Black, American actress
  - Elise Testone, American singer-songwriter
  - Tania Gunadi, Indonesian-American actress and producer
  - Inés Gómez Mont, Mexican television host, reporter and actress
- July 30 – Seán Dillon, Irish footballer
- July 31 – Kim Moylan, Irish actress

August

Robin van Persie

Chris Hemsworth

Mila Kunis

Andrew Garfield

Jamala

- August 2 – Huston Street, American baseball player
- August 3
  - Mamie Gummer, American actress
  - Michelle Buswell, American model
- August 4
  - Mariusz Wlazły, Polish volleyball player
  - Adhir Kalyan, South African actor

- o Greta Gerwig, American actress and filmmaker
- o Jai Crawford, Australian cyclist
- August 5 – Kara Tointon, English actress
- August 6 – Robin van Persie, Dutch footballer
- August 7
  - o Brit Marling, American actress, screenwriter and producer
  - o Maggie Castle, Canadian actress
  - o Tina O'Brien, British actress
  - o Christian Chávez, Mexican singer and actor
- August 9
  - o Sarah Elizabeth, American model
  - o David Ames, British actor
  - o Ashley Johnson, American actress
- August 10
  - o Spencer Redford, American actress
  - o Mathieu Roy, Canadian professional ice hockey player
- August 11
  - o Chris Hemsworth, Australian actor
  - o Sammy Glenn, English television actress
- August 13
  - o Aleš Hemský, Czechoslovakian ice hockey player
  - o Sebastian Stan, Romanian-born American actor
- August 14
  - o Elena Baltacha, Ukrainian-Scottish tennis player (d. 2014)
  - o Mila Kunis, Ukrainian/American actress
  - o Spencer Pratt, American television personality
- August 16 – Nikos Zisis, Greek basketball player
- August 17 – Dustin Pedroia, American baseball player
- August 18
  - o Mika, Lebanese-British singer
  - o Cameron White, Australian cricketer
  - o Kris Boyd, Scottish football player
- August 19
  - o Tammin Sursok, Australian actress
  - o Claudia Salinas, Mexican model and actress

- o Missy Higgins, Australian pop singer-songwriter, musician and actor
- o Tania Nolan, New Zealand actress
- o Reeva Steenkamp, South African model (d. 2013)
- August 20
  - o Yuri Zhirkov, Russian footballer
  - o Andrew Garfield, British/American actor
- August 21
  - o Brody Jenner, American television personality
  - o Chantelle Houghton, English glamour model and television personality
- August 23
  - o Ruta Gedmintas, Lithuanian-English actress
  - o Annie Ilonzeh, American actress
  - o James Collins, Welsh footballer
- August 24 – Brett Gardner, American baseball player
- August 27
  - o Jamala, Ukrainian singer and songwriter, Eurovision Song Contest 2016 winner
  - o Wilson Chen, Taiwanese actor
- August 28 – Lasith Malinga, Sri Lankan cricketer
- August 29 – Jennifer Landon, American actress
- August 30 – Jun Matsumoto, Japanese singer and actor
- August 31
  - o Larry Fitzgerald, American football player
  - o Maria Flor, Brazilian actress

September

Maggie Grace

Amy Winehouse

Donald Glover

Andreea Raducan

- September 1
    - José Antonio Reyes, Spanish football player
    - Camille Mana, American actress
- September 2 – Tiffany Hines, American television actress and singer
- September 3
    - Valdas Vasylius, Lithuanian basketball player
    - Alexander Klaws, German singer
- September 4 – Jennifer Metcalfe, English actress
- September 5 – Priscilla Meirelles, Miss Earth 2004
- September 8 – Chris Judd, Australian rules footballer
- September 9 – Zoe Kazan, American actress and screenwriter
- September 10
    - Joey Votto, Canadian baseball player
    - Filip Bandžak, Czech opera singer, baritone
- September 11 – Vivian Jepkemoi Cheruiyot, Kenyan long-distance runner
- September 12 – Carly Smithson, Irish singer
- September 13 – Kaoklai Kaennorsing, Thai Muay Thai kickboxer
- September 14 – Amy Winehouse, British singer (d. 2011)
- September 15 – Ashleigh McIvor, Canadian freestyle skier
- September 16 – Kirsty Coventry, Zimbabwean swimmer
- September 17
    - Catherine Tyldesley, English actress and model

- o Jennifer Peña, American singer
- September 18
  - o Kevin Doyle, Irish footballer
  - o Sasha Son, Lithuanian singer
- September 20
  - o Yuna Ito, American-Japanese singer and actress
  - o A-Lin, Taiwanese singer
- September 21
  - o Maggie Grace, American actress
  - o Joseph Mazzello, American actor
  - o Sarah Rees Brennan, Irish novelist
  - o Anna Meares, Australian track cyclist
- September 22 – Eriko Imai, Japanese singer (Speed)
- September 23 – Märt Israel, Estonian discus thrower
- September 24
  - o Randy Foye, American basketball player
  - o Lyndon Ferns, South African swimmer
- September 25
  - o Donald Glover, American actor
  - o Son Dam-bi, South Korean singer
- September 26 – Ricardo Quaresma, Portuguese footballer
- September 27 – Jeon Hye-bin, South Korean actress and singer (LUV)
- September 28
  - o Sarah Wright, American actress
  - o Julissa Bermudez, Dominican American television personality and actress
- September 30
  - o Andreea Răducan, Romanian gymnast
  - o Reiko Shiota, Japanese badminton player

October

Jesse Eisenberg

Loreen

Kıvanç Tatlıtuğ

- October 1 – Anna Drijver, Dutch actress and model
- October 2 – Gerran Walker, American football player
- October 3
  - Hiroki Suzuki, Japanese actor
  - Meghan Heffern, Canadian actress
  - Tessa Thompson, American actress
- October 4
  - Risa Kudō, Japanese gravure idol
  - Shontelle, Barbadian singer, and songwriter
  - Vicky Krieps, Luxembourgish actress
- October 5
  - Jesse Eisenberg, American actor
  - Nicky Hilton, American model and socialite
  - Noah Segan, American character actor
  - Noot Seear, Canadian fashion model and actress
- October 8
  - Michael Fraser, Scottish football goalkeeper
  - Lou Charmelle, French pornographic actress

- October 9 – Spencer Grammer, American actress
- October 10 – Alyson Hau, Hong Kong radio DJ
- October 11 – Bradley James, English actor
- October 13 – Katia Winter, Swedish actress
- October 14
  - Lin Dan, Chinese badminton player
  - Zesh Rehman, English-Pakistani footballer
  - David Oakes, English film, television and theatre actor
- October 15 – Stephy Tang, Hong Kong singer and actress
- October 16 – Loreen, Swedish pop singer and music producer, Eurovision Song Contest 2012 winner
- October 17
  - Daniel Kajmakoski, Macedonian singer and songwriter
  - Ivan Saenko, Russian footballer
  - Daniel Booko, American actor
  - Felicity Jones, English actress
- October 19
  - Cara Santa Maria, American neuroscientist and writer
  - Rebecca Ferguson, Swedish model and actress
- October 20 – Alona Tal, Israeli television actress
- October 21
  - Charlotte Sullivan, Canadian actress
  - Ashley Banjo, Canadian actor
  - Marie Marguerite, Duchess of Anjou, Venezuelan heiress and wife of Louis Alphonse of Bourbon, Duke of Anjou
  - Aaron Tveit, American actor
- October 24
  - Brian Vickers, American race car driver
  - Katie McGrath, Irish actress
  - Ashleigh Harrington, Canadian actress
  - V V Brown, English singer, songwriter, model, and producer
  - Adrienne Bailon, American singer and actress
- October 25 – Princess Yōko of Mikasa, member of the Japanese Imperial Family

- October 27
    - Kıvanç Tatlıtuğ, Turkish actor and model
    - Dmitri Sychev, Russian footballer
    - Katy Tur, American journalist
- October 29
    - Amit Sebastian Paul, Swedish singer (A*Teens)
    - Johnny Lewis, American actor (d.2012)
- October 30 – Diana Karazon, Jordanian singer

November

Philipp Lahm

Adam Driver

Professor Green

- November 1
  - Yuko Ogura, Japanese gravure idol
  - Jelena Tomašević, Serbian pop singer
- November 3 – Julie Marie Berman, American actress
- November 5 – Alexa Chung, English television presenter and model
- November 4 – Tyler Everett, American football player
- November 7 – Lauren Elaine, American fashion designer, model and actress
- November 8
  - Pavel Pogrebnyak, Russian footballer
  - Blanka Vlašić, Croatian high jumper
- November 9 – Meseret Defar, Ethiopian long-distance runner
- November 10 – Miranda Lambert, American country music singer
- November 11
  - Philipp Lahm, German footballer
  - Kristal Marshall, American professional wrestler, model and beauty queen
  - Sola Aoi, Japanese model
  - Tatsuhisa Suzuki, Japanese voice actor
- November 12 – Kate Bell, Australian actress
- November 15 – Laura Smet, French actress
- November 16 – K, Korean singer
-

- November 17
  - Viva Bianca, Australian actress
  - Ioannis Bourousis, Greek basketball player
  - Ryan Bradley, American figure skater
  - Ryan Braun, American baseball player
  - Évelyne Brochu, Canadian actress
  - Harry Lloyd, British actor
  - Nick Markakis, American baseball player
  - Rocsi, American television personality
- November 18
  - Jon Johansen, Norwegian computer programmer
  - Robert Kazinsky, English actor and model
- November 19
  - Adam Driver, American actor
  - DeAngelo Hall, American football player
  - Daria Werbowy, Ukrainian-Canadian model
- November 20
  - Future, American rapper, singer, and songwriter
  - Angel De-Mar, American Musician, singer and songwriter
- November 22 – Tyler Hilton, American singer-songwriter and actor
- November 24
  - Dean Ashton, British footballer
  - José López, Venezuelan baseball player
- November 25 – Atsushi Itō, Japanese actor
- November 27 – Professor Green, British rapper
- November 28
  - Courtney Rush, Canadian professional wrestler
  - Ellie Taylor, English comedian and television presenter
  - Kelly Wenham, English actress
- November 29
  - Jenn Sterger, American television personality and model
  - Aylin Tezel, German actress
- November 30 – Nicholas Kole, American figure skater

December

Jennifer Hawkins

Jonah Hill

- December 2
  - Mette Lindberg, Danish singer
  - Bibiana Candelas, Mexican volleyball player
  - Ana Lucía Domínguez, Columbian actress
  - Jana Kramer, American actress
  - Aaron Rodgers, American football player
  - Daniela Ruah, Portuguese actress
- December 3
  - Troy Bergeron, American football player
  - Andy Grammer, American singer/songwriter
- December 4
  - Jimmy Bartel, Australian rules footballer

- o Charity Shea, American actress
- o Roman Zaretsky, Israeli figure skater
- December 5
  - o Tori Sparks, American singer/songwriter and activist
  - o Tiffany Weimer, American footballer
- December 6 – Francesca Jackson, English musical theatre actress
- December 7 – Fausto Carmona, Dominican baseball player
- December 9 – Dariusz Dudka, Polish footballer
- December 10
  - o Patrick Flueger, American actor
  - o Xavier Samuel, Australian actor
- December 12 – Katrina Elam, American singer
- December 13
  - o Satya Bhabha, British actor
  - o Otylia Jędrzejczak, Polish swimmer
  - o J Alvarez Puerto Rican singer
- December 15
  - o René Duprée, Canadian professional wrestler
  - o Wang Hao, Chinese table tennis player
  - o Brooke Fraser, New Zealand folk-pop and Christian musician
  - o Camilla Luddington, English actress
- December 16 – Danielle Lloyd, British model
- December 17 – Erik Christensen, Canadian hockey player
- December 19
  - o Nektarios Alexandrou, Cypriot footballer
  - o AJ Lamas, American actor
  - o Casey Crescenzo, American singer-songwriter and guitarist (The Dear Hunter and The Receiving End of Sirens)
  - o Bridget Phillipson, English politician
  - o Laura Pomeroy, Canadian swimmer
  - o Matt Stajan, Canadian ice hockey player
- December 20
  - o Jonah Hill, American actor
  - o Lucy Pinder, English model
  - o Lara Stone, Dutch model
  - o Nelly Alisheva, Russian volleyball player

- December 22
  - Jennifer Hawkins, Australian television personality, Miss Universe 2004
  - Joe Dinicol, Canadian actor
  - Nathalie Péchalat, French ice dancer
- December 23 – Hanley Ramírez, Dominican baseball player
- December 25 – Gwei Lun-Mei, Taiwanese actress
- December 27 – Cole Hamels, American baseball player
- December 28 – Aiko Nakamura, Japanese tennis player
- December 29 – Jessica Andrews, American country music singer

Date unknown

- Linda Bhreathnach, Irish television actress
- Kristi Capel, American beauty pageant and news presenter
- Sarah Earnshaw, British actress
- Yalda Hakim, Australian journalist
- Lisa Hammond, English actress
- Leila Benn Harris, English actress and singer
- Eleonore Hendricks, American actress, photographer and casting director
- Ainsley Howard, British actress
- Mari Lövgreen, Welsh television presenter
- Jane McGregor, Canadian actress
- Ashley Austin Morris, American actress
- Daráine Mulvihill, Irish television personality
- Sophy Ridge, British journalist and Political Correspondent for Sky News
- Brook Roberts, American television personality and former beauty pageant
- Fernanda Romero, Mexican actress and model
- Roxy Shahidi, English actress
- Zoe Tuckwell-Smith, Australian actress

Deaths

January

Louis de Funès

Juan Carlos Zabala

- January 2 – Dick Emery, British comedian (b. 1915)
- January 8 – Gerhard Barkhorn, German World War II fighter ace (b. 1919)
- January 10 – Roy DeMeo, American Mafia hitman (b. 1942)
- January 11
  - Ghanshyam Das Birla, Indian industrialist and educator (b. 1894)

- o Tikhon Kiselyov (also Kiselev), Belarusian statesman in the Soviet Union, the de facto leader of the Byelorussian SSR from 1980 to 1983 (b. 1917)
- January 12 – Nikolai Podgorny, Ukrainian politician, Chairman of the Presidium of the Supreme Soviet of the USSR from 1965 to 1977 (b. 1903)
- January 13 – David M. Shoup, American general (b. 1904)
- January 15
  - o Masatane Kanda, Japanese general (b. 1890)
  - o Meyer Lansky, American gangster (b. 1902)
- January 17 – Doodles Weaver, American comedian and uncle of Sigourney Weaver (b. 1911)
- January 23 – Fred Bakewell, English cricketer (b. 1908)
- January 24
  - o George Cukor, American film director (b. 1899)
  - o Juan Carlos Zabala, Argentine athlete (b. 1911)
- January 26 – Paul "Bear" Bryant, American college football coach (b. 1913)
- January 27
  - o Georges Bidault, French Resistance leader (b. 1899)
  - o Michael "Pat" Bilon, American dwarf actor (b. 1947)
  - o Louis de Funès, French actor (b. 1914)
- January 28
  - o Frank Forde, fifteenth Prime Minister of Australia (b. 1890)
  - o Billy Fury, British musician (b. 1940)
- January 29 – Stuart H. Ingersoll, American admiral (b. 1898)

February

Karen Carpenter

Tennessee Williams

- February 4 – Karen Carpenter, American singer and drummer (b. 1950)
- February 8 – Harry Boot, English physicist (b. 1917)
- February 12 – Eubie Blake, American musician and songwriter (b. 1887)
- February 14 – Lina Radke, German athlete (b. 1903)
- February 19 – Alice White, American actress (b. 1904)
- February 22 – Sir Adrian Boult, English conductor (b. 1889)
- February 23 – Herbert Howells, English composer (b. 1892)
- February 25 – Tennessee Williams, American playwright (b. 1911)
- February 27 – Nikolai Aleksandrovich Kozyrev, Russian astronomer and astrophysicist (b. 1908)
- February 28 – Winifred Atwell, British pianist (b. 1914)

March

Rebecca West

Umberto II of Italy

- March 1 – Hideo Kobayashi, Japanese author (b. 1902)
- March 3
    - Hergé, Belgian comics creator (b. 1907)
    - Arthur Koestler, Austrian writer (b. 1905)
- March 6 – Donald Maclean, British spy (b. 1913)
- March 7 – Igor Markevitch, Ukrainian conductor (b. 1912)
- March 8 – William Walton, English composer (b. 1902)
- March 9
    - Faye Emerson, American actress (b. 1917)
    - Ulf von Euler, Swedish physiologist, Nobel Prize laureate (b. 1905)
- March 14 – Maurice Ronet, French film actor and director (b. 1927)
- March 15 – Rebecca West, English-born writer (b. 1892)

- March 16
  - Arthur Godfrey, American radio and television broadcaster and entertainer (b. 1903)
  - Freda Dudley Ward, former royal mistress (b. 1894)
- March 17 – Haldan Keffer Hartline, American physiologist, Nobel Prize laureate (b. 1903)
- March 18
  - Umberto II of Italy, the last King of Italy (b. 1904)
  - Ivan Vinogradov, Russian mathematician (b. 1891)
- March 25 – Bob Waterfield, American football player (Los Angeles Rams) and a member of the Pro Football Hall of Fame (b. 1920)
- March 26 – Anthony Blunt, British spy and art historian (b. 1907)
- March 27
  - Elsie Eaves, American civil engineer (b. 1898)
  - James Hayter, British actor (b. 1907)
- March 30 – Lisette Model, Austrian-born American photographer (b. 1901)

April

Gloria Swanson

- April 3 – Jimmy Bloomfield, English football player and manager (b. 1934)
- April 4
  - Jacqueline Logan, American actress (b. 1901)
  - Gloria Swanson, American actress (b. 1899)
- April 11 – Dolores del Río, Mexican actress (b. 1905)
- April 12 – Desmond Bagley, English novelist (b. 1923)

- April 15
  - Corrie ten Boom, Dutch resistance fighter (b. 1892)
  - Gyula Illyés, Hungarian poet and novelist (b. 1902)
- April 19 – Jerzy Andrzejewski, Polish author (b. 1909)
- April 20
  - Walther Nehring, German general (b. 1892)
  - Pedro Quartucci, Argentine boxer and actor (b. 1905).
- April 21 – Walter Slezak, Austrian actor (b. 1902)
- April 22 – Earl 'Fatha' Hines, American musician (b. 1903)
- April 23
  - Buster Crabbe, American actor and athlete (b. 1908)
  - Selena Royle, American actress (b. 1904)
  - Alberto Zorrilla, Argentine Olympic swimmer (b. 1906)
- April 30
  - George Balanchine, Russian choreographer (b. 1904)
  - Joel Henry Hildebrand, American chemist (b. 1881)
  - Muddy Waters, American musician (b. 1915)

May

Jack Dempsey

- May 1
  - George Hodgson, Canadian Olympic swimmer (b. 1893)
  - Joseph Ruttenberg, Russian-born cinematographer (b. 1889)
  - Arthur D. Struble, American admiral (b. 1894)
- May 2 – Norm Van Brocklin, American football player (Los Angeles Rams) and coach (Minnesota Vikings) and a member of the Pro Football Hall of Fame (b. 1926)
- May 5 – John Williams, British actor (b. 1903)

- May 8 – John Fante, American writer (b. 1909)
- May 14 – Roger J. Traynor, American judge (b. 1900)
- May 15 – James Van Der Zee, American photographer (b. 1886)
- May 18 – Frank Aiken, Irish Foreign Minister (b. 1898)
- May 19 – Jean Rey, President of the European Commission (b. 1902)
- May 21 – Kenneth Clark, British art historian (b. 1903)
- May 22
  - Albert Claude, Belgian biologist, recipient of the Nobel Prize in Physiology or Medicine (b. 1899)
  - King Idris of Libya (reigned from 1951 to 1969) (b. 1889)
- May 25 – Sid Daniels, British merchant marine worker, last surviving crewmember of the RMS *Titanic* dies (b. 1895)
- May 29 – Arvīds Pelše, Latvian historian, Soviet politician and functionary (b. 1899)
- May 31 – Jack Dempsey, American heavyweight champion boxer (b. 1895)

June

Norma Shearer

- June 1 – Prince Charles of Belgium (b. 1903)
- June 2 – Stan Rogers, Canadian musician (b. 1949)
- June 8 – Miško Kranjec, Slovenian writer (b. 1908)
- June 10 – Larry Hooper, American singer (b. 1917)
- June 12 – Norma Shearer, Canadian-born actress (b. 1902)
- June 15 – Srirangam Srinivasarao, also known as Sri Sri, Telugu poet (b. 1910)

- June 17 – Peter Mennin, American composer and teacher (b. 1923)
- June 18
  - Robert Riddles, British locomotive engineer (b. 1892)
  - Marianne Brandt, German industrial designer (b. 1893)
- June 23 – Osvaldo Dorticós Torrado, 21st President of Cuba (suicide) (b. 1919)
- June 24 – Charles Phelps Taft II, American politician, son of President William Howard Taft (b. 1897)
- June 25 – Alberto Ginastera, Argentine composer (b. 1916)
- June 30 – Mary Livingstone, American comedian (b. 1905)

July

Buckminster Fuller

- July 1 – Buckminster Fuller, American architect (b. 1895)
- July 4
  - Dr John Bodkin Adams, British suspected serial killer (b. 1899)
  - Ted Berrigan, American poet (b. 1934)
- July 5 – Harry James, American musician and band leader (b. 1916)
- July 7
  - Herman Kahn, American futurist (b. 1922)
  - Vicki Morgan, American model (murdered) (b. 1952)
- July 9 – Keith Wickenden, British politician (b. 1932)
- July 10 – Werner Egk, German composer (b. 1901)
- July 11 – Ross Macdonald, American-Canadian writer (b. 1915)
- July 12 – Chris Wood, British rock musician (b. 1944)

- July 15 – Eddie Foy, Jr., American actor (b. 1905)
- July 16 – Samson Raphaelson, American screenwriter (b. 1894)
- July 17 – Roosevelt "Honeydripper" Sykes, American blues musician (b. 1906)
- July 19 – Erik Ode, German actor (b. 1910)
- July 20 – Frank Reynolds, American journalist (b. 1923)
- July 23 – Georges Auric, French composer (b. 1899)

David Niven

- July 26
  - Larry Gains, Canadian boxer (b. 1901)
  - Charlie Rivel, Spanish Catalan circus clown (b. 1896)
- July 29
  - Luis Buñuel, Spanish-born filmmaker (b. 1900)
  - Raymond Massey, Canadian actor (b. 1896)
  - David Niven, English actor (b. 1910)
- July 30
  - Howard Dietz, American lyricist (b. 1896)
  - Lynn Fontanne, British actress (b. 1887)

August

Carolyn Jones

Benigno Aquino Jr.

- August 1
  - Peter Arne, British actor (b. 1920)
  - Lilian Mercedes Letona, Salvadoran guerrilla (b. 1954)
- August 2 – James Jamerson, American musician (b. 1938)
- August 3
  - Carolyn Jones, American actress (b. 1930)
  - Jobriath, American musician and actor (b. 1946)
- August 5 – Judy Canova, American actress (b. 1913)
- August 6 – Klaus Nomi, German singer and performance artist (b. 1944)
- August 16 – Earl Averill, American baseball player (Cleveland Indians) and a member of the MLB Hall of Fame (b. 1902)
- August 17 – Ira Gershwin, American lyricist (b. 1896)
- August 18 – Nikolaus Pevsner, German-born art historian (b. 1902)
- August 21 – Benigno Aquino, Jr., Filipino politician (b. 1932)
- August 27 – Harry A. deButts, American railroad executive
- August 28 – Jan Clayton, American actress (b. 1917)
- August 29 – Simon Oakland, American actor (b. 1915)

September

- September 1
  - Larry McDonald, American politician (plane crash – KAL 007 victim) (b. 1935)

- ○ Henry M. "Scoop" Jackson, American politician (aortic aneurysm after giving a news conference condemning the shooting down of KAL 007) (b. 1912)

Felix Bloch

- September 10
  - ○ Felix Bloch, Swiss-born physicist, Nobel Prize laureate (b. 1905)
  - ○ Jon Brower Minnoch, heaviest man who ever lived (b. 1941)
  - ○ Dai Rees, British golfer (b. 1913)
  - ○ B. J. Vorster, Prime Minister of South Africa (b. 1915)
- September 12 – Sabin Carr, American Olympic athlete (b. 1904)
- September 17 – Humberto Sousa Medeiros, Cardinal Archbishop of Boston between 1970 and 1983 (b. 1915)
- September 20 – Ángel Labruna, Argentine footballer and manager (b. 1918)

Léopold III of Belgium

- September 25 – King Léopold III of Belgium (b. 1901)
- September 26 – Tino Rossi, Corsican singer (b. 1907)
- September 26 – Possibly everyone in the world, if not for the actions (or rather inaction) of a certain Russian.
- September 29 – Alan Moorehead, Australian-born English war correspondent and historian (b. 1910)

October

- October 5 – Earl Tupper, American businessman (b. 1907)
- October 6 – Terence Cooke, Cardinal Archbishop of New York (b. 1921)
- October 8 – Joan Hackett, American actress (b. 1934)
- October 10
  - Georgia Cozzini, American socialist politician (b. 1915)
  - Ralph Richardson, British actor (b. 1902)
- October 14 – Paul Fix, American actor (b. 1901)
- October 15 – Pat O'Brien, American actor (b. 1899)
- October 18 – Willie Jones, baseball player (b. 1925)
- October 19 – Maurice Bishop, Grenadian politician and revolutionary (b. 1944)
- October 20 – Peter Dudley, British actor (b. 1935)
- October 21 – Joseph P. Lordi, American government official (b. 1919)
- October 23
  - Jessica Savitch, American journalist (b. 1947)
  - Toru Takahashi, Japanese race car driver (b. 1960)
- October 26 – Mike Michalske, American football player (Green Bay Packers) and a member of the Pro Football Hall of Fame (b. 1903)
- October 28
  - Roderick Gill, Irish cricketer (b. 1919)
  - Otto Messmer, American cartoonist (b. 1892)
- October 31 – George S. Halas, American football player and coach (Chicago Bears), a co-founder of the National Football League, and a member of the Pro Football Hall of Fame (b. 1895)

November

- November – Barney Bubbles, English graphic artist (b. 1942)
- November 3 – Alfredo Antonini, American conductor and composer (b. 1901)
- November 7 – Germaine Tailleferre, French composer (b. 1892)
-

- November 8
  - Robert Agnew, American actor (b. 1899)
  - Betty Nuthall, English tennis champion (b. 1911)
- November 13 – Junior Samples, American comedian (b. 1926)
- November 14 – Tómas Guðmundsson, Icelandic poet (b. 1901)
- November 15 – John Le Mesurier, British actor (b. 1912)
- November 19 – Carolyn Leigh, American lyricist (b. 1926)
- November 20
  - Marcel Dalio, French actor (b. 1900)
  - Richard Loo, Chinese-American actor (b. 1903)
- November 23 – Waheed Murad, Legendary Pakistani actor, film producer, writer and director (b. 1938)
- November 25 – Michael Conrad, American actor (b. 1925)
- November 28 – Christopher George, American actor (b. 1931)
- November 30 – Richard Llewellyn, British writer (b. 1906)

December

Mir Gul Khan Nasir

Joan Miró

Dennis Wilson

- December 2 – Fifi D'Orsay, Canadian actress (b. 1904)
- December 4 – Bobby Goodman, U.S. Navy A-6 Intruder Bombardier Navigator shot down over Lebanon; captured upon ejection and held captive in Syria for 30 days; pilot Mark Lange died of injuries
- December 5 – Robert Aldrich, American film director (b. 1918)
- December 6 – Lucienne Boyer, French singer (b. 1903)
- December 6 – Gul Khan Nasir, Baloch politician and poet from Pakistan (b. 1914)
- December 8
  o Keith Holyoake, New Zealand politician, 26th Prime Minister of New Zealand (b. 1904)
  o Slim Pickens, American actor (b. 1919)
- December 9 – David Rounds, American actor (b. 1930)
- December 11 – Sir Neil Ritchie, British general (b. 1897)
- December 13
  o Leora Dana, American actress (b. 1923)
  o Mary Renault, English author (b. 1905)
- December 15 – David Markham, British actor (b. 1913)
- December 21
  o Paul de Man, Belgian-born literary critic (b. 1919)
  o Rod Cameron, American actor (b. 1910)
- December 23 – Colin Middleton, Northern Irish artist (b. 1910)
- December 25 – Joan Miró, Catalan painter (b. 1893)
- December 26 – Violet Carson, British actress (b. 1898)
- December 27 – William Demarest, American actor (b. 1892)

- o Walter Scott, American performer (b. 1943)
- December 28
  - o Dennis Wilson, American singer, songwriter and drummer (b. 1944)
  - o Jimmy Demaret, American golf champion (b. 1910)

Date unknown

- Mary Cohan, Broadway composer and lyricist, daughter of George M. Cohan (b. 1909)

Nobel Prizes

- Physics – Subrahmanyan Chandrasekhar, William Alfred Fowler
- Chemistry – Henry Taube
- Medicine – Barbara McClintock
- Literature – William Golding
- Peace – Lech Wałęsa
- Economics – Gérard Debreu

In the News

Seatbelt use for drivers and front seat passengers becomes mandatory in the United Kingdom.

The Worlds Population is estimated at 4.72 billion.

The United States invades Grenada.

Richard Noble sets a new land speed record of 633.468 mph, driving Thrust 2 at the Black Rock Desert, Nevada.

Brinks Mat warehouse robbery at Heathrow Airport making off with three tons of gold bars valued at $37.5 million.

The first mobile phones, are introduced to the public by the Motorola Company.

Breakfast TV starts in UK with the BBC Breakfast Time and TV-am.

Sally Ride on June 18th becomes first American woman in space on the Space Shuttle Challenger.

Margaret Thatcher wins landslide victory in General Elections in the UK.

The children's show "Fraggle Rock" debuts on HBO as one of the premium cable network's first original programs.

Microsoft Word is first released.

Popular Films - Star Wars Episode VI: Return of the Jedi, Tootsie, Trading Places, WarGames, Superman III, Flashdance, Staying Alive, Octopussy, National Lampoon's Vacation.